We Have a Government

Ann Bonwill

Content Consultant

Elizabeth Case DeSantis, M.A. Elementary Education
Julia A. Stark Elementary School, Stamford, Connecticut

Reading Consultant

Jeanne M. Clidas, Ph.D.
Reading Specialist

Children's Press®
An Imprint of Scholastic Inc.

Library of Congress Cataloging-in-Publication Data

Names: Bonwill, Ann, author.
Title: We have a government/by Ann Bonwill.
Description: New York, NY: Children's Press, an imprint of Scholastic Inc., 2019. |
Series: Rookie read-about civics | Includes index.
Identifiers: LCCN 2018030275 | ISBN 9780531129166 (library binding) |
ISBN 9780531137741 (pbk.)
Subjects: LCSH: Political science—United States—Juvenile literature. |
Executive power—United States—Juvenile literature.
Classification: LCC JA70 .B66 2019 | DDC 320.973—dc23

Produced by Spooky Cheetah Press
Design: Keith Plechaty/kwpCreative
Creative Direction: Judith E. Christ for Scholastic Inc.

Published in 2019 by Children's Press, an imprint of Scholastic Inc.

Printed in North Mankato, MN, USA   113

SCHOLASTIC, CHILDREN'S PRESS, ROOKIE READ-ABOUT®, and associated logos are trademarks and/or registered trademarks of Scholastic Inc.

1 2 3 4 5 6 7 8 9 10 R 28 27 26 25 24 23 22 21 20 19

Scholastic, Inc., 557 Broadway, New York, NY 10012.

Photographs ©: cover: KidStock/Getty Images; cover background: emyu/iStockphoto; cover flag bunting: LiveStock/Shutterstock; 3: DCornelius/Shutterstock; 4: Monkey Business Images/Shutterstock; 7: Paul Morse/White House/Getty Images; 9 tree: Shendart/iStockphoto; 9 buildings: JPL Designs/Shutterstock; 10: Alistair Berg/Getty Images; 13: Andy Cross/Getty Images; 15 inset: BigAlBaloo/Shutterstock.com; 15: miralex/iStockphoto; 16: Alex Wong/Getty Images; 16 background: Elenamiv/Shutterstock; 19: U.S. Navy/Getty Images; 21: NextNewMedia/Shutterstock; 22: DEA PICTURE LIBRARY/Getty Images; 23: Chones/Shutterstock; 24: rusm/iStockphoto; 25: Everett Historical/Shutterstock; 27: Jamie Grill/Getty Images; 28: Elyse Lewin/Getty Images; 29: My Life Graphic/Shutterstock; 30 top left: Chris Parypa Photography/Shutterstock; 30 top right: MarciSchauer/Shutterstock; 30 bottom left: Niyazz/Shutterstock; 30 bottom right: foto-select/Shutterstock; 30 background: Big Foot Productions/Shutterstock; 30 frames: Chinch/Shutterstock; 30 top paper: Lukiyanova Natalia frenta/Shutterstock; 31 top right: Paul Morse/White House/Getty Images; 31 center right inauguration: Alex Wong/Getty Images; 31 center right judge: sebra/Shutterstock; 31 bottom right: Drop of Light/Shutterstock.

Table of Contents

CHAPTER 1

Working Together

It takes a lot of people to make a school run well. Teachers, custodians, and the principal each have a part to play. They all work together to help the school run smoothly.

 How does your teacher make your class run smoothly?

The same can be said for our country's government. Different people in the government work together to make our country run smoothly. Just like in a school!

Why is it important for our country's government to run smoothly?

The president meets with advisers in the Oval Office.

The United States government is made up of three main parts, called branches. The **legislative** branch makes laws. The **judicial** branch helps us understand what those laws mean. The **executive** branch makes sure the laws are followed. The president of the United States is the leader of the executive branch.

Who is the president of the United States?

The Three Branches of Government

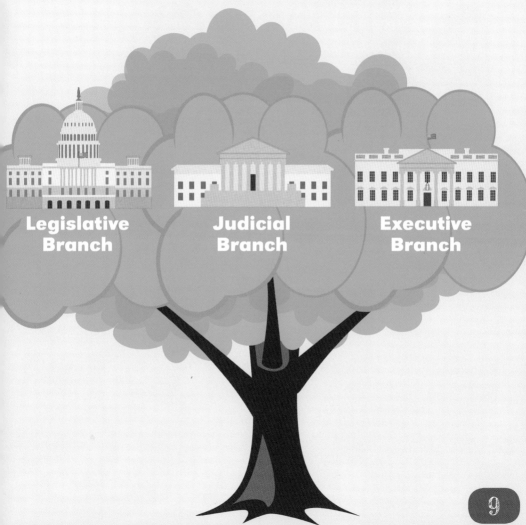

Legislative Branch

Judicial Branch

Executive Branch

CHAPTER 2

Leaders in Charge

Our parents are the leaders of our family. Our principal is the leader of our school. Our government has many different leaders. We listen to our leaders. We respect what they say.

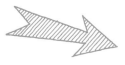 Who is the leader of your sports team?

A mayor is the leader of a town or city.
A governor is the leader of a state.
They are our local leaders.

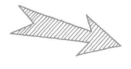 Who is the mayor
of your town
or city?

This class got a visit from their city's mayor.

The president is one of our national leaders. Adults vote for a new president every four years.
A president can be elected only two times in a row.

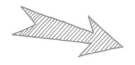 Have you ever gone to vote with an adult?

The president lives in the White House in Washington, D.C.

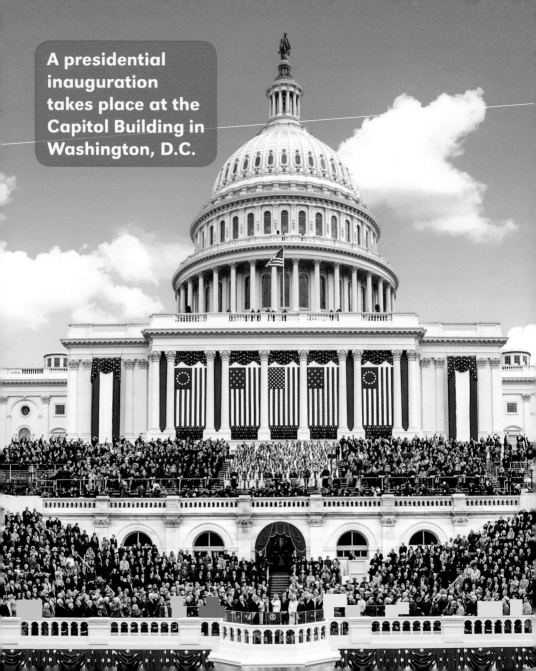

A presidential inauguration takes place at the Capitol Building in Washington, D.C.

CHAPTER 3

Presenting the President!

After the president is elected, there is an **inauguration**. There are parties and parades to celebrate. Then the president and the president's family move to the White House.

Who was our first president?

The president says yes or no to new laws. He or she recommends how to spend the country's money. He or she chooses people to do important jobs in the government. The president is also in charge of our armed forces, such as the army and navy. He or she makes many speeches to share plans and ideas.

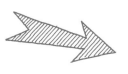 What ideas would you share if you were the president?

The navy operates on the sea. These service members are marching on the deck of an aircraft carrier.

The president works with other countries, too. He or she flies on a plane called Air Force One. Being the president is a difficult job with a lot of important duties.

 Why does the president need a special plane?

CHAPTER 4

Learning from Leaders

One of our country's greatest leaders was George Washington. He was our first president. Our nation's capital, Washington, D.C., is named after him.

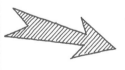 Whose face do you see on a dollar bill?

Abraham Lincoln was our 16th president. He was also a great leader. Lincoln was born in a log cabin and liked to read and learn. He worked hard to make sure all Americans could be free.

 Whose face do you see on a penny?

Like Washington and Lincoln, strong leaders listen to and help others. They set a good example with their words and actions. We need great leaders in our government. People in our government lead our country and shape our world.

 How can you be a leader in school?

Why is it important to have good leaders?

Do You Know the

The Pledge of Allegiance is a promise to be loyal to the United States. The Pledge of Allegiance was written for children in 1892. Now adults also say the Pledge to show respect for America and its flag. You probably say the Pledge in school. But do you know what all the words mean?

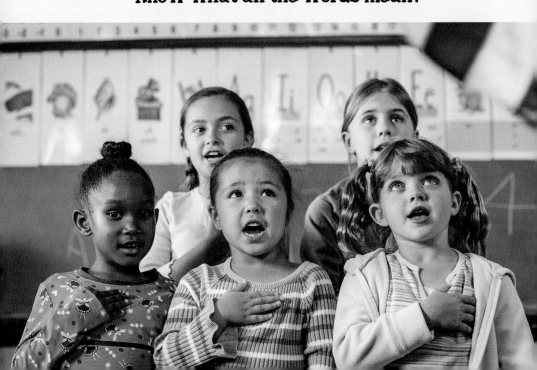

Pledge of Allegiance?

I pledge **allegiance** ← "Allegiance" means loyalty.

to the Flag

of the United States of America,

and to the **Republic** ← In a republic, citizens vote for their leaders. The United States is a republic.

for which it stands,

one Nation under God,

This means that the country can't be split apart. → **indivisible**,

with liberty and justice for all.

The last line means that every citizen is free and will be treated fairly.

American Symbols

These are four symbols that represent the
American ideals of freedom and strength.

Statue of Liberty
(New York City, New York)

Bald Eagle

American Flag

Liberty Bell
(Philadelphia, Pennsylvania)

executive (ig-**zek**-yuh-tive): **the branch of government that carries out the laws of the United States**
▶ *The president is the head of the* **executive** *branch.*

inauguration (in-aw-gyuh-**ray**-shuhn): **ceremony of swearing in a public official**
▶ *After the president is elected, there is an* **inauguration**.

judicial (joo-**dish**-all): **having to do with a court of law or a judge**
▶ *The* **judicial** *branch helps us understand our laws.*

legislative (**lej**-is-lay-tiv): **the branch of the government that makes laws**
▶ *The* **legislative** *branch makes laws.*

Index

Facts for Now

Visit this Scholastic website for more information on our government:

www.factsfornow.scholastic.com

Enter the keyword **Government**

About the Author

Ann Bonwill enjoys writing books for children. She lives with her husband and son in northern Virginia, not far from the White House.